MW00678035

Dear God, Please Help Me Stay On My Diet Today

Dear God, Please Help Me Stay On My Diet Today

A Spiritual Approach to Weight Loss for Those Who Love God

Written by Gail M. Freid
Illustrated by Gail M. Freid

Published by Creative Visions Publishing Co.
Oak Park, Michigan

Dear God, Please Help Me Stay On My Diet Today
A Spiritual Approach to Weight Loss for Those Who Love God
Published by Creative Visions Publishing Co.

http://www.CreativeVisionsPublishing.com
http://www.SpiritualDietSeminars.com

Editorial supervision: Lynn Lombardo, and Paulette Lerman
Formatting: Jason Hammond

Publishers Note:

This book is written as a source of information only, and is not a substitute for the advice of a qualified medical professional. We urge you to consult with your physician before changing any exercise or weight loss program.

All efforts have been made to ensure the accuracy of the information contained in this book. The author and publisher expressly disclaim responsibility for any adverse effects arising from the use or application of the information contained within.

All rights reserved. No part of this book may be reproduced by any mechanical, photographic, or electronic process, or in the form of phonographic recording; nor may it be stored in a retrieval system, transmitted, or otherwise be copied for public or private use—other than for "fair use" as brief quotations embodied in articles and reviews—without prior written permission of the publisher.

The intent of the author is only to offer information to help you in your quest for emotional, physical, and spiritual well-being. The publisher and author assume no responsibility for your actions.

Copyright © 2009 by Gail M. Freid
ISBN: 978-0-9823460-0-6
Library of Congress Cataloging-in-Publication Data Pending

For my children, Audrey and Jacqueline,
and all of our furry babies
that keep us in Spirit

Acknowledgments

I must offer my gratitude first to Reverend Jack Boland, the Minister and Founder of The Church of Today Unity in Warren, Michigan. I first heard Jack's voice on the telephone where he recorded a daily message of inspiration. After I experienced spiritual enlightenment, he was the first person to say all the things I was thinking. I visited the church and knew I was home. I learned much from this man of God and am so grateful to have known and loved him. I keep his spirit in my heart.

I also wish to thank my two dear friends that I have known since Junior High School. Debra Feldman's devotion and love for me always keeps me going on every project I birth. Paulette Lerman's support for this endeavor kept my head from exploding in handling the details that made me crazy.

There is also my High School English teacher, Ruth Clay, who told the class that students really can be smart, even if they don't get "A"s on everything. So, instead of becoming a beautician, I became an English teacher and discovered I *was* smart.

I want to thank Marianne Williamson, who I think has one of the most brilliant minds on our planet today. She taught me that brilliant people can be devoted to God, and she spoke about it every Sunday at The Church of Today, now called Renaissance Unity.

To my daughter, Audrey, who lost 45 pounds from sheer will-power and a lot of exercise, and keeps me motivated to eat vegetables. To my daughter, Jackie, who is enthusiastic about everything and gives me inspiration and hope.

To all the people who have touched my life and have moved on, thank you for the pleasure and the pain of growth.

And now I thank my readers who have put their trust in me to bring something of value to their lives.

A Beautiful Table Set With Many Contents

INTRODUCTION

God heard your prayers and passed them on to me. You know, the prayers where you asked for help and guidance for staying on your diet and losing weight. So, here it is!

Dear God, Please Help Me Stay On My Diet Today
A Spiritual Approach to Weight Loss
for Those Who Love God

It is not a diet book. It is not a cook book. There are no low-fat recipes to make or calories to count. It is not Biblical. It is not even going to discuss the obesity epidemic in America.

This book is about providing you with a very powerful support system that will keep you on your "diet of choice" to find hope and success, while improving your health and life. This sometimes serious, sometimes funny book is about allowing your spirituality to crack through your destructive eating habits. It addresses the problem that every dieter faces time after time; the failed results which keep the unhealthy and overweight person feeling defeated and hopeless.

While pondering this problem, I finally figured out that if God could create the entire universe with all of its intricacies and wonder; if this powerful and loving God could create all the creatures in the ocean and all the creatures of the Earth; if He could build the mountains, form the galaxies, the planets, and the stars, He could certainly help me stay on a diet.

While struggling with my own weight and health issues, I began writing prayers and keeping them in my purse to read while waiting somewhere. As I wrote, the prayers multiplied, bloomed, and morphed into reminders about food, God's gifts, self-realization, discipline, Spirit, activities, and just for fun. I laughed about stories of the dreaded scale and sneaking ice cream, and how we Americans eat standing over the sink. Then I made a list of all the things I could do instead of eating. It was exhilarating. Inspiration and excitement took over and the book was born.

There are six sections in the book.

- The first section is devoted to the reminders I call, Miraculously Memorable Minders™. They are extremely easy to remember because they are succinct and meaningful, giving us ammunition to fight our battle with food. The Minders will pop into your mind at every choice you make all day long, such as:

"Smaller plates, smaller portions, smaller you."

- The second section is a collection of light stories related to dieting and food that we all share in common. There are funny poems, and an important essay on finding your passion.

- The third section is a collection of prayers to get us through the day without cheating or giving up. This is the part of the book that will give hope to the frustrated dieter who has struggled forever. This, alone, makes the book invaluable because you can take it with you wherever you go. With the prayers, you gain a deeper relationship with God, knowing that His Power is with you from morning, throughout the day, and until you fall into bed at night.

- The fourth section is on keeping a journal. This will help keep you on track and responsible to your program. It is yours alone, and you can write about your feelings, struggles, and joys. You are the author of your life. Write it down.

- The fifth section is devoted to Bunches of Things to Do Besides Eating. We must have projects to keep us busy and occupied and away from the refrigerator. There are lots to choose from. You may even find a passion or an avocation among the list of activities.

- The sixth section offers related reading and websites for your support. The author's credentials are included.

My Mission Statement

It is my passion to create a book about

finding a healthy lifestyle, a hopeful future,

a stronger spirituality, and abundance for

those who are struggling with weight issues

by honoring and relying on God,

however one understands God to be.

My Spiritual Path

By the age of twelve, I had decided that God could not possibly exist and that I never wanted to get married. I witnessed violent discourse between my parents and knew when I grew up, I wanted none of that. A teacher had our class write an essay on whether we thought people were inherently good or inherently evil. I picked evil.

I reached college age during the era that chanted the phrase, "God is dead". I think that we, who grew up in the 50's and 60's, recognized social hypocrisy. Good God-fearing people were fighting another war and killing more young men. Being young and without wisdom, we thought we could make a better world by "making love, not war". While we were making love, they were making war. I guess our message of love wasn't clear enough or loud enough.

It was also a time when women wanted their independence and to be self-reliant, and men got all confused and didn't know what women wanted them to do. I remember a nice gentleman holding a door open for me, and I took offense because he should have known that I could certainly open a door for myself. He kindly said, "You first," and I said, "No, you first." And giving it another try, he said, "No you first," as I repeated, "No, you first," until he threw up his hands, grunted, and in his frustration, shaking his head, went through the door.

I did marry a college professor who loved a good argument and was a critic of everything. Being in a college environment, it was fashionable to be an intellectual atheist, and we held every card. We were always in debate with someone who believed in God and couldn't prove it. Science was the ruler of the day, so we knew we were on the "right" side. I even had a science professor who claimed there was no such thing as instinct. He was certain that all creature behavior was learned. So, my mantra was, "God is dead. God is dead. God is dead."

Then life happened to me along the way and I didn't like it one bit. I got divorced and was caring for two young children with no help at all. I developed a really bad attitude. My then boyfriend wanted to get married, and I knew that wasn't going to happen, so he left and found someone who would. I was very alone. So, I went to sleep for about three months.

While in my self-induced prison, I watched television. A preacher caught my eye. I noticed his face was peaceful and he was smiling like no one I had ever seen. He mesmerized me and I couldn't stop watching him. I saw this peace in his eyes and decided I wanted what he had. He said all I had to do was surrender my will to God, and I would find peace. I was resistant for a long time, while holding on to my intellectual views, but on one really, really bad day, I surrendered. While crying and screaming, I took a red lipstick and wrote on the wall, "I surrender to the Power of the Universe." I surrender. And there it was on my wall--my release. My release from who I was, to who I would become.

From that moment, I became God's child. Everything was new. I was brand new. This weird unfamiliar feeling came over me. It seriously flip-flopped my brain. I got up. I was shaky and I could barely walk. I looked at everything with new eyes. I went outside to see the flowers of the Earth for the first time. They were so beautiful and colorful and bright and brilliantly creative. Only a Power so loving could make those flowers. I looked at the clouds and felt the breeze. I lay down in the grass. I could not believe how the world suddenly looked through my rose-colored glasses. God created everything, and it was all mine to explore and to enjoy. God did that for me. My mind and heart were over-flowing with feelings of love, and flowers began growing out of my head.

Oh my God, thank you for this magnanimous world. I'm so sorry for not knowing You and for arguing against You. Oh my God, please forgive me. I love You. You are beautiful and to be exalted. You are mine. I am yours. I bow to Your Will.

That was the beginning of my spiritual journey. It has taken me to many wonderful and peaceful places and connected me with many wonderful and peaceful people. I have been a student for almost 30 years and, while always a student, I am now ready to become the teacher.

Part One

Miraculously Memorable Minders™

Miraculously Memorable Minders™

According to Wikipedia, a **minder** is, "a person assigned to guide or escort a visitor, or to provide protection to somebody or to otherwise assist or take care of something." The concept works for our purposes.

Miraculous Memorable Minders™ are short memorable thoughts and reminders about food and Spirit that are remarkably effective in developing control over eating. They are effective because we can remember and recite them as if they were little rhymes, like those from our childhood.

Instead of:
Peter Piper picked a peck of pickled peppers,

A Miraculously Memorable Minder™ is:

Put pepper on the party food
and push the plate away.

There are several categories: Food, God's Gifts, Self-Realization, Discipline, Spirit, Activities, and Just for Fun.

The food section offers reminders about food, while taking God into consideration. They are the things we think about all day long when we're hungry, bored, or stressed. It's about making positive healthy choices.

God's Gifts are about the foods that God has given us for our sustenance and pleasure, the beauty and colors of Planet Earth, and our God-given bodies.

Self-Realization presents ideas on one's worth as a loving creation of God. It's about taking care of ourselves and others, and the freedom to be who God created us to be.

Discipline concerns the ways we can get our thinking straight in order to reach the goals we've set for ourselves. Discipline is about getting what we want. Discipline is about the hope and freedom to finally love our bodies and ourselves.

Spirit is about us and recognizing and honoring God in our lives and our deepening relationship with Him.

Activities are the fun things we can do to keep our minds off of food.

I have designed the Miraculously Memorable Minders™ section as a workbook, so that you can explore your thoughts and emotions in response to each one. You might also write a memory associated with a Miraculously Memorable Minder™. It is important to work with these associations because, when a Miraculously Memorable Minder™ pops into your head during the day, you will have a broader understanding of how to deal with emotional, unconscious eating. It is a strong tool for you to use toward your success. You will discover that all of the Miraculously Memorable Minders™ make a connection with God, and that is the strongest tool of all.

With Spirit and success,

Gail M. Freid

FOOD

What Does This Mean To You?
Food

Smaller plate,
smaller portions,
smaller you.

My response to reading this is that I must make a conscious decision to take a smaller plate before I put anything on it. Another conscious choice I must make is to take a portion size that is half, or less than I normally take. Only by eating mindfully with cautious choices will I be able to lose weight and become healthier. I feel sad or angry that I cannot have everything I want when I want it. But, I know that becoming a more responsible person will help me become the person I want to be. I will also be demonstrating to my family and friends that I am taking care of myself, because I am worthy of health. It will be a teaching and learning experience for others, as well. I will be passing the example on, or "paying it forward".

An experience I had that relates to food is when I went shopping one day at a fruit market. Someone asked me how to eat the persimmon I was holding. We had a conversation about it, and I learned that he actually had a persimmon tree in his backyard in California. I thought of having my own persimmon tree and dreaming of a warm and sunny backyard in summer. Persimmons are an exotic fruit and most people don't buy them because they look rotten when they are ripe for eating. If you do not know that, and you buy them when they look firm and solid, they taste absolutely horrible. You must allow them to ripen with black bruises, and they must be very soft and mushy. Then they are sweet and delicious and ready to eat. I love them and always buy them when they are in season. Try one as a sweet treat.

What Does This Mean To You?
Food

_____
_____
_____
_____
_____
_____
_____
_____
_____
_____
_____
_____
_____
_____
_____
_____
_____
_____
_____
_____
_____
_____
_____

The more veggies,
the less of you.

You *know* what
makes you fat.
Don't eat it.

You *can* have
one bite, one taste,
one piece, a smidge.

What Does This Mean To You?
Food

_____

_____

_____

_____

_____

_____

_____

_____

_____

_____

_____

_____

_____

_____

_____

_____

_____

_____

_____

_____

_____

_____

_____

_____

_____

_____

Drink cool, clean water
to purify and cleanse your body
for health and healing.

Smaller plate,
smaller portions,
smaller you.

Eating less food
gives you more energy.

What Does This Mean To You?
Food

_____

_____

_____

_____

_____

_____

_____

_____

_____

_____

_____

_____

_____

_____

_____

_____

_____

_____

_____

_____

_____

_____

_____

_____

Less calories
help you to
feel better and live longer.

Don't drink
your calories.

Healthy choices
are God's choices.

What Does This Mean To You?
Food

_____

_____

_____

_____

_____

_____

_____

_____

_____

_____

_____

_____

_____

_____

_____

_____

_____

_____

_____

_____

_____

_____

_____

_____

_____

You can't eat all the time
and be healthy and thin.

The supermarket is
God's Garden of Eden.
It is not the stuper-market.
Abundance is yours.

If you don't like a food that is healthy,
take a spoonful to develop a taste.
It's a "no thank you" helping.

What Does This Mean To You?
Food

_____

_____

_____

_____

_____

_____

_____

_____

_____

_____

_____

_____

_____

_____

_____

_____

_____

_____

_____

_____

_____

_____

_____

_____

Take a piece of fruit in hand.
Acknowledge its purity,
wholesomeness,
and gift.
Understand its sacredness.
Give thanks,
and eat.

Fiber sweeps out
the colon and
keeps you clean and light.

A good question to ask is,
"Does God grow it?"

What Does This Mean To You?
Food

_____

_____

_____

_____

_____

_____

_____

_____

_____

_____

_____

_____

_____

_____

_____

_____

_____

_____

_____

_____

_____

_____

_____

_____

_____

_____

If you think you should eat it,
then do.
If you think you shouldn't eat it,
then don't.

Study the orange.
Each section is a cluster of
tender, juicy teardrops
all protected by
a fabulous, colorful, thick skin.

Healthy snacks between meals
keep you from being too hungry.

What Does This Mean To You?
Food

_____

_____

_____

_____

_____

_____

_____

_____

_____

_____

_____

_____

_____

_____

_____

_____

_____

_____

_____

_____

_____

_____

_____

Fresh
is better than frozen.
Frozen
is better than canned.

Be conscious. Be mindful.
Think *before*
popping it in your mouth.

Sugars and fats
make you sick.
They clog up your arteries.

What Does This Mean To You?
Food

_____

_____

_____

_____

_____

_____

_____

_____

_____

_____

_____

_____

_____

_____

_____

_____

_____

_____

_____

_____

_____

_____

_____

_____

_____

_____

Fill the fridge only
with God's natural bounty.
Natural food is
God's prescription for your health.

Eat lots of carrots, celery, and apples.
They will keep your mouth busy.
Crunch, crunch, crunch.

You know your food weaknesses.
You know your food strengths.
Eat with this knowledge in mind.

What Does This Mean To You?
Food

_____

_____

_____

_____

_____

_____

_____

_____

_____

_____

_____

_____

_____

_____

_____

_____

_____

_____

_____

_____

_____

_____

_____

_____

Healthy, frozen dinners
are measured and counted.
No brainers.

Starchy foods like white potatoes,
white rice, white pasta, white bread,
will make you fat, fat, fat.

It's either fattening,
or it's not.
There is no bargaining.

What Does This Mean To You?
Food

_____

_____

_____

_____

_____

_____

_____

_____

_____

_____

_____

_____

_____

_____

_____

_____

_____

_____

_____

_____

_____

_____

_____

_____

_____

_____

_____

_____

EAT FISH

Make a huge pot
of fresh vegetable soup,
and eat as much as you want.

Bathe your fruits and vegetables
with loving care.
Water, soap, and towel dry.

What Does This Mean To You?
Food

_____

_____

_____

_____

_____

_____

_____

_____

_____

_____

_____

_____

_____

_____

_____

_____

_____

_____

_____

_____

_____

_____

Nurture a tomato plant
in the spring.
Harvest tomatoes
in the fall.
Share the bounty.

Take smaller bites.
Nibble, nibble, nibble.
Slowly.

Salads are green and full of
colorful natural foods
provided for you to enjoy.

What Does This Mean To You?
Food

_____

_____

_____

_____

_____

_____

_____

_____

_____

_____

_____

_____

_____

_____

_____

_____

_____

_____

_____

_____

_____

_____

_____

When at the movies,
pass the popcorn and candy counter
and just keep walking.

It could have been worse.
You could have eaten
the whole cake.

Eating Holy foods
nourishes your body and
brings you closer to God.

What Does This Mean To You?
Food

_____

_____

_____

_____

_____

_____

_____

_____

_____

_____

_____

_____

_____

_____

_____

_____

_____

_____

_____

_____

_____

_____

_____

_____

You don't need to
even it out.

Go toward the
lite.

When offered a mint,
take only one.

Drink vegetable juice
with lemon.
It's tasty and healthy.

What Does This Mean To You?
Food

_____

_____

_____

_____

_____

_____

_____

_____

_____

_____

_____

_____

_____

_____

_____

_____

_____

_____

_____

_____

_____

_____

_____

_____

_____

"Eat, drink, and be merry,
for tomorrow you may die."

or

Eat good food,
drink pure water,
and care for yourself,
or tomorrow you may die.

Give thanks
for your bounty.
You are blessed and have
everything you need.

GOD'S GIFTS

What Does This Mean To You?
God's Gifts

When I think of all that God has given us, I am overwhelmed. The beauty and colors of nature are the first things that come to mind. God's magnanimous world, in all its splendor, surrounds us every moment that we breathe.

> Look up to the sky, clouds, sun, moon,
> stars, planets, and endless universe.
> Look down to the depths of the ocean
> and its amazing aquatic life.
> Look straight ahead to see the trees,
> mountains, lakes, and beautiful creatures.
> The intricacies of the world
> are God's gifts.

The poem is simple and brief, but God's world is deep and full of wonder. It is color and texture and beauty and life. Everything on Earth is moving and interacting and changing in every moment. You are also in movement as you dance the dance of your life.

When you look at nature or food or your body, you can choose to see God within all, and embrace the Source as part of your life. If you choose the leap of faith, you know that you are a miracle of God's love. You can then choose to live your life for that loving Spirit.

I saw a television show in which a physician was doing a heart transplant in a baby. They had taken a healthy heart from a baby who died, and they froze it to transport it to the hospital. The physician removed the unhealthy heart from the sick baby and replaced it with the healthy heart that had defrosted. It began to beat and send life blood through the child. This man of science looked at the camera, pulled down his mask and said, "It never ceases to amaze me when a heart begins to beat on its own. It's an absolute miracle."

You are a miracle and one of God's gifts. Live well and dance.

What Does This Mean To You?
God's gifts

_____

_____

_____

_____

_____

_____

_____

_____

_____

_____

_____

_____

_____

_____

_____

_____

_____

_____

_____

_____

_____

_____

_____

_____

_____

_____

God is an artist.
He created all the colors
and all the flowers
for you to enjoy.

God is
goodness and creativity.

Celebrate the
beautiful, healthy body
you've been given.
Keep it well.

What Does This Mean To You?
God's gifts

_____
_____
_____
_____
_____
_____
_____
_____
_____
_____
_____
_____
_____
_____
_____
_____
_____
_____
_____
_____
_____
_____
_____
_____
_____

You deserve the best.
You deserve all
that God has
to give.

God will never
give up on you.
Don't give up on Him.

God's natural world
is quiet.
Turn off the electronics
and listen for Him.

What Does This Mean To You?
God's gifts

_____

_____

_____

_____

_____

_____

_____

_____

_____

_____

_____

_____

_____

_____

_____

_____

_____

_____

_____

_____

_____

_____

_____

The most beautiful
things in nature are
God's gifts to you.

God is the Creator
of all that is.
He made you.

Because He lovingly created you,
you are worthy.
Treat yourself with respect.

What Does This Mean To You?
God's gifts

_____

_____

_____

_____

_____

_____

_____

_____

_____

_____

_____

_____

_____

_____

_____

_____

_____

_____

_____

_____

_____

_____

_____

_____

_____

If God can create
the mountains and the seas,
He can help you stay on a diet.

Making excuses
denies God's power.

Light and love
surround you
at every decision.

What Does This Mean To You?
God's gifts

_____

_____

_____

_____

_____

_____

_____

_____

_____

_____

_____

_____

_____

_____

_____

_____

_____

_____

_____

_____

_____

_____

_____

_____

Surround yourself
with beauty
every day.

God blessed us
with sexual desires.
Enjoy what He has given.
It burns calories, too.

Isn't it amazing!
God made jackets for
happy sweet corn kernels.

What Does This Mean To You?
God's gifts

_____

_____

_____

_____

_____

_____

_____

_____

_____

_____

_____

_____

_____

_____

_____

_____

_____

_____

_____

_____

_____

_____

_____

_____

Sunflower seeds are
God's gift presented by
sunny flowers.

Isn't it amazing
how grapes
hang out in groups?

Isn't it amazing!
God made pods for peas
to grow in.

What Does This Mean To You?
God's gifts

_____
_____
_____
_____
_____
_____
_____
_____
_____
_____
_____
_____
_____
_____
_____
_____
_____
_____
_____
_____
_____
_____
_____
_____

Fruit trees
are God's great gift to you.
Plant some.

Look up to the sky, clouds, sun, moon,
stars, planets, and endless universe.

Look down to the depths of the ocean
and its amazing aquatic life.

Look straight ahead to see the trees,
mountains, lakes, and beautiful
creatures.

The intricacies of the world
are God's gifts.

SELF-REALIZATION

What Does This Mean To You?
Self-realization

Growth comes
as you move through
uncomfortable change.
It is safe.

Change is usually uncomfortable, even if it is for the better. Change can be fearful. By this time in my life, I know my fears cannot lead me around. I remind myself that I am making up stories in my head, and that I couldn't possibly know what will happen until it actually happens, and then it is open to interpretation. The made-up mind games and worries we put on ourselves are fantasies, not realities.

Self-realization is about making choices with conscious intention so that our lives become what we want them to be. Choices are risky and scary. Growth is a tough master that will not allow you to remain stagnant. Change is inevitable.

I ask myself, am I unhappy with where I am, or who I am, or do I want more? Do I want to become healthy, strong, and possibly deliriously happy? Yes, yes, and yes! So, I must embrace change and the possibilities of growth; the probability of growth.

Every moment is a new beginning
to turn it all around.
Begin again.

I know I must work as hard as I can to make the changes I want. It's not easy, but with God standing by my side, I know I have the support I need. Not just support, but my Divine birthright to happiness as a child of God. I cannot do it on my own, but with the greatest Power that is, I can do it with Him.

What Does This Mean To You?
Self-realization

_____

_____

_____

_____

_____

_____

_____

_____

_____

_____

_____

_____

_____

_____

_____

_____

_____

_____

_____

_____

_____

_____

_____

_____

_____

Growth comes
as you move through
uncomfortable change.
It is safe.

Every moment is
a new beginning
to turn it all around.
Begin again.

Your time on Earth
is precious.
Use it well and for good.

What Does This Mean To You?
Self-realization

_____

_____

_____

_____

_____

_____

_____

_____

_____

_____

_____

_____

_____

_____

_____

_____

_____

_____

_____

_____

_____

_____

_____

_____

There is so much
wonderful
waiting for you.
Go get it.

Forgive yourself
for the past.
You can create a new life
without shame.

Your diet toward health
can be your private secret
with God.

What Does This Mean To You?
Self-realization

_____
_____
_____
_____
_____
_____
_____
_____
_____
_____
_____
_____
_____
_____
_____
_____
_____
_____
_____
_____
_____
_____
_____
_____
_____
_____
_____
_____
_____

Your thoughts *are* your world.
Be careful what you say
to yourself.

You are what you think about.
Think about good things.

Make room in your life
for you.

What Does This Mean To You?
Self-realization

_____

_____

_____

_____

_____

_____

_____

_____

_____

_____

_____

_____

_____

_____

_____

_____

_____

_____

_____

_____

_____

_____

_____

_____

_____

_____

You didn't blow it.
Simply start over from now.

Show compassion
to others,
for you are one of them.

There is always
a first step.
Take it,
as God holds your hand.

What Does This Mean To You?
Self-realization

_____

_____

_____

_____

_____

_____

_____

_____

_____

_____

_____

_____

_____

_____

_____

_____

_____

_____

_____

_____

_____

_____

_____

_____

It gets better and easier
as you go through it.

Choose joy.
Do the things you love.

Laugh
as often as possible.

Doing good things
for your body
gives thanks to God.

What Does This Mean To You?
Self-realization

_____

_____

_____

_____

_____

_____

_____

_____

_____

_____

_____

_____

_____

_____

_____

_____

_____

_____

_____

_____

_____

_____

_____

_____

_____

_____

_____

Be honest and trustworthy
and a person of integrity.
It can be contagious.

Do not take on
other people's fears and doubts.
They don't belong to you.

You are powerful.
You create and re-create yourself
moment by moment.

What Does This Mean To You?
Self-realization

_____
_____
_____
_____
_____
_____
_____
_____
_____
_____
_____
_____
_____
_____
_____
_____
_____
_____
_____
_____
_____
_____
_____
_____
_____
_____

Be conscious and present
at all times.
WAKE UP.

Find your passion.
Become immersed in
something you love to do.

You have always done
the best you could at the time.
You can do better now.

What Does This Mean To You?
Self-realization

_____

_____

_____

_____

_____

_____

_____

_____

_____

_____

_____

_____

_____

_____

_____

_____

_____

_____

_____

_____

_____

_____

_____

_____

_____

_____

_____

_____

_____

Share your secrets
only with those who are supportive,
or in need of your help.

You are becoming stronger
and more gentle.

Accomplishments lead to
self-esteem.
Accomplishments lead to
strength of mind.

What Does This Mean To You?
Self-realization

_____

_____

_____

_____

_____

_____

_____

_____

_____

_____

_____

_____

_____

_____

_____

_____

_____

_____

_____

_____

_____

_____

_____

_____

Be a person who
can be trusted.
Trust yourself.

Do something wonderful
for someone else.

When you learn to
love yourself,
you will drop *toxic* people.

What Does This Mean To You?
Self-realization

What you think about expands.
Expand the good stuff.
Be in touch with your Spirit.

The sky has no boundaries;
God has no limitations.
Look up.

Complaining and whining
are not becoming
for a child of God.

What Does This Mean To You?
Self-realization

_____

_____

_____

_____

_____

_____

_____

_____

_____

_____

_____

_____

_____

_____

_____

_____

_____

_____

_____

_____

_____

_____

_____

_____

_____

It feels good to feel well.
Make positive changes
and love yourself.

Your thoughts are your own.
You decide which ones to share.

Be all that you can be
for yourself
and God.

What Does This Mean To You?
Self-realization

_____

_____

_____

_____

_____

_____

_____

_____

_____

_____

_____

_____

_____

_____

_____

_____

_____

_____

_____

_____

_____

_____

_____

_____

Growth is maturity,
relaxing into yourself,
making new choices,
knowing you're okay.

Maturity is
letting go of your dreams,
then taking them back.

You are God's special soul
to stand with Him
in wonderfulness.

DISCIPLINE

What Does This Mean To You?
Discipline

Losing 20 pounds or
gaining 20 pounds
are both possible.
It's your decision.

Discipline is about getting our thinking centered so that we make the *careful* decisions that are going to get us to where we want to be. I know that I am the one who controls my weight. I know that I am the one who contributes to my health. I know that I talk to myself about whether or not to eat that éclair or a half gallon of ice cream. All these thoughts in my head are talking and fighting with me all day long. Doctor Seuss' fictitious character, the "push-me-pull-you", lives in my head. Eat it, don't eat it. It looks so good. Are you *trying* to get fatter? I want it, I want it. No, you don't. I am making choices and decisions constantly throughout the day.

I also know that if I talk to God and take Him into consideration when making my choices, then my choices will be more *carefully and sensibly thought through.* If I read the Miraculously Memorable Minders™ and prayers every day or several times a day, they will remind me that I can ask God to be a partner in my choices. I will be able to achieve the disciplined mind I am seeking.

Decide now.
Forever fat,
forever thin.
Forever sick,
forever healthy.

My choice is forever healthy, forever joyful, forever your servant.

What Does This Mean To You?
Discipline

_____

_____

_____

_____

_____

_____

_____

_____

_____

_____

_____

_____

_____

_____

_____

_____

_____

_____

_____

_____

_____

_____

_____

_____

_____

_____

_____

Losing 20 pounds or
gaining 20 pounds
are both possible.
It's your decision.

It's never too late,
unless you're dead.

Before deciding spontaneously,
count to 20, breathe, and ask,
"Do I want to change my life?"

What Does This Mean To You?
Discipline

_____

_____

_____

_____

_____

_____

_____

_____

_____

_____

_____

_____

_____

_____

_____

_____

_____

_____

_____

_____

_____

_____

_____

_____

_____

Self-sabotage is,
"Just this once."

Commit to getting through
the next 15 minutes,
then the next 15 minutes.
Do something productive.
Don't just sit there.

Your choices are always your own.
Always and only yours.

What Does This Mean To You?
Discipline

_____

_____

_____

_____

_____

_____

_____

_____

_____

_____

_____

_____

_____

_____

_____

_____

_____

_____

_____

_____

_____

_____

_____

_____

_____

_____

_____

Eat when you're hungry,
Stop when you're full.
Not stuffed.

You don't have to eat it all right now.
Eat some now and
save the rest for another time.

NO PICKING

You had your treat.
Now STOP!

What Does This Mean To You?
Discipline

_____

_____

_____

_____

_____

_____

_____

_____

_____

_____

_____

_____

_____

_____

_____

_____

_____

_____

_____

_____

_____

_____

_____

_____

Put pepper on the
party food and
push the plate away!

Structure your eating day.
Plan your meals and snacks.

Only you have control
over your eating.

Say, "No thank you"
and leave it at that.

What Does This Mean To You?
Discipline

_____

_____

_____

_____

_____

_____

_____

_____

_____

_____

_____

_____

_____

_____

_____

_____

_____

_____

_____

_____

_____

_____

_____

_____

_____

_____

Discipline is
nurtured training
for a self-controlled mind.

Act responsibly.
That's what adults do.

Be an example
for your children and others.
You pass it on.

You can do it.
You're developing
strength of character.

What Does This Mean To You?
Discipline

_____

_____

_____

_____

_____

_____

_____

_____

_____

_____

_____

_____

_____

_____

_____

_____

_____

_____

_____

_____

_____

Breaking bad habits
gives you integrity.

Change the places where you eat.
Make a "no negotiating" rule.
No eating in the car after shopping.
No eating at the office.
No eating over the sink.
No eating in bed.
Eating is allowed at the table,
sitting down with plates and silverware.

Commit to losing
2 pounds at a time.

What Does This Mean To You?
Discipline

_____
_____
_____
_____
_____
_____
_____
_____
_____
_____
_____
_____
_____
_____
_____
_____
_____
_____
_____
_____
_____
_____
_____
_____
_____

You are in control
of your own life.
Weigh your decisions.

Decide now.
Forever fat,
forever thin.
Forever sick,
forever healthy.

Just for the next hour.
Just for this morning.
Just for this afternoon.
Just for this evening.
Just for today.

What Does This Mean To You?
Discipline

_____
_____
_____
_____
_____
_____
_____
_____
_____
_____
_____
_____
_____
_____
_____
_____
_____
_____
_____
_____
_____
_____
_____
_____
_____
_____
_____
_____

Action changes everything.
Go into action, now.

Decide to change
one bad habit this week.
Write it down and keep it with you.

Success is
one pound at a time.

What Does This Mean To You?
Discipline

_____

_____

_____

_____

_____

_____

_____

_____

_____

_____

_____

_____

_____

_____

_____

_____

_____

_____

_____

_____

_____

_____

_____

_____

_____

_____

You *know* how
to do it.

Think things through
carefully.
Then decide.

Just STOP!
That's all.
Just STOP!

What Does This Mean To You?
Discipline

_____

_____

_____

_____

_____

_____

_____

_____

_____

_____

_____

_____

_____

_____

_____

_____

_____

_____

_____

_____

_____

_____

_____

If not now, when?
The past is only a memory,
the future is only imagined.
The only time to make changes
is NOW, not later.

If you have to think about
"should I or shouldn't I eat it",
the answer is always, "NO".

Throw it out.
You don't have to finish it.

What Does This Mean To You?
Discipline

_____

_____

_____

_____

_____

_____

_____

_____

_____

_____

_____

_____

_____

_____

_____

_____

_____

_____

_____

_____

_____

_____

_____

_____

_____

_____

_____

Develop a taste for
goodness.

Make certain you're hungry
before you eat.

Any diet will do,
if you do the diet.

Eat a big breakfast.
Eat a mid-size lunch.
Eat a small dinner.

What Does This Mean To You?
Discipline

_____

_____

_____

_____

_____

_____

_____

_____

_____

_____

_____

_____

_____

_____

_____

_____

_____

_____

_____

_____

_____

_____

_____

_____

_____

_____

_____

_____

Don't bring it into
the house.

If it's in the house,
throw it out.

Don't weigh.
Just *stay* on the diet.

Eat before you
shop for food.

What Does This Mean To You?
Discipline

_____

_____

_____

_____

_____

_____

_____

_____

_____

_____

_____

_____

_____

_____

_____

_____

_____

_____

_____

_____

_____

_____

_____

_____

_____

_____

Have half as much
and save the rest for
tomorrow.

It's simple.
You don't need it.

In the end, God will say,
"Well done, my child, well done."
And He won't be talking
about steak!

SPIRIT

What Does This Mean To You?
Spirit

Spirit is about us and our deepening relationship with God. Over the years, I have questioned my faith. I promised God I would never separate from Him again, yet I have wavered. I believe this is a natural human quality for one who is an independent thinker. In order to be authentic, we need to question and get clear on what our feelings and thoughts are concerning our faith. As I go through this process and commit to loving God so deeply, I know it is real. When I am in my present Spirit-mind, answers come to me.

Thirty years ago, when I surrendered my mind and heart to God, a passion to learn everything I could about Spirit and religions engaged me. I began to read and research and listen to all the authors and speakers who were sharing their experiences and thoughts about what they knew.

I was introduced to the Church of Today by an orthodox Jewish friend of mine who put me on the telephone to listen to Reverend Jack Boland's *Unity thought-for-the-day.* I visited the church and fell in love with all it had to offer. The church had a bookstore filled with books and tapes on many things I wanted to know about: spirituality, spiritual leaders, relationships, prayer, and life challenges. I devoured as much as I could take in. ***It was my spiritual food.***

During this time, I felt as though a silver strand was attached from my heart reaching to the heavens. I believed this to be an umbilical cord from me to God. As I felt like a newborn child, I believed my Holy Father was not going to let me go. That feeling stayed with me every moment of every day for one full year. Then, as a parent must cut the cord, I was gently pushed into the world to explore. It was safe in my new world, and I felt protected. As an actual child, I remember the feeling when my biological father held me; I knew nothing could ever harm me. I wrapped my small arms around his neck and put my head on his shoulder. I was safe and comforted.

Many of the things that happen to us seem to be odd coincidences. I look at them as though God is a movie director. There was an incident I thought was so funny. My young children and I were shopping in a mall, and we were approaching a store corner. Unaware to us, on the other side of the store approaching the same corner was their cousin whom they hadn't seen for years. As children will do, my youngest turned around to talk to me while still walking backwards. At the same time, her cousin had also turned to talk to her mother and was walking backwards. And, boom! They backed into each other like a choreographed dance. What a strange coincidence. I saw God whirling his finger and laughing.

I live in Michigan, and one winter it had not stopped snowing since the beginning of December. I feared that it would continue all season. I usually enjoyed shoveling and blowing the snow myself and considered it my exercise for the day. However, the temperatures had fallen below zero and it was really cold outside. I just kept staring out of the window and sighing. The snow was at least two feet deep and I did not want to shovel. My mailman will not deliver my mail if the walks are not cleared off. Since the next day was Sunday, I decided to wait until the morning to brave the cold.

Late that night my doorbell rang and there appeared three young angels with shovels, who were about to earn their wings. Now, you may not consider that a miracle, but I did. In thirty years, no one has come by to shovel unless the snow was a half inch deep and the temperature was 40 degrees as the snow was melting. Ting-a-ling went the bell, (from the Christmas movie, "It's a Wonderful Life"). If you think that was just a coincidence, I have another story to tell.

One day, I was in the kitchen with the whole family making lunch. I commented that I wondered why the Girl Scouts never come around anymore selling cookies. They used to come every year, but no longer do. The doorbell rang, and guess who was at the door with an order form. Yes, it was a Girl Scout! Cookies! My kids said I was spooky. It's a true story.

As I write this essay on Spirit, I am watching the Presidential Inauguration of Barack Obama where 1.5 million people listening to him speak stand in the cold in perfect silence with so much hope. It is the day that follows the holiday of Dr. Martin Luther King Jr. who **had a dream** that "people should be judged on the strength of their character, and not on the color of their skin." This is an overwhelmingly emotional day for our country.

Some time ago, I was waiting in the big fat cinnamon bun line at the airport with my travel partner. The bun was for him, not for me. I did not know who was standing in front of me. A young woman came up to the gentleman in line and asked for his autograph. When she left, I touched his shoulder and quietly said, "Excuse me, who are you?" He said that he was Martin Luther King Jr.'s son. Tears welled up in my eyes and I could hardly speak. As I held my hands over my heart, I told him I was honored to be standing next to him, and that I felt a Holy Presence.

I asked him if I could touch the back of his coat, and he said I could. I touched his back between his shoulder blades. This is the support spot of the spine where we seem to carry a lot of stress. Touching or massaging that spot seems to give comfort and both people share in its energy. It took all my control not to burst into tears. When he got his cinnamon bun, he turned to me, nodded with a smile, understanding my feelings, and left. For me, there was a Holy Presence.

With Spirit, I feel protected, missing cousins bump into each other, angels show up with shovels, Girl Scouts show up with order forms for cookies, dreams come to pass, and miracles happen.

What Does This Mean To You?
Spirit

_____

_____

_____

_____

_____

_____

_____

_____

_____

_____

_____

_____

_____

_____

_____

_____

_____

_____

_____

_____

_____

_____

_____

_____

Be *hungry* for God,
and *full* of spirit.

You radiate
beauty and goodness
because you are.

Either you have faith
or you don't.
If you do,
then live what you believe.

What Does This Mean To You?
Spirit

_____

_____

_____

_____

_____

_____

_____

_____

_____

_____

_____

_____

_____

_____

_____

_____

_____

_____

_____

_____

_____

_____

_____

_____

You are a part of the
"All That Is".
You are a part of God.

God gave you intuition.
Tune in.

There are no limitations
with God.
Limits are self-imposed.

What Does This Mean To You?
Spirit

_____

_____

_____

_____

_____

_____

_____

_____

_____

_____

_____

_____

_____

_____

_____

_____

_____

_____

_____

_____

_____

_____

_____

_____

_____

God will always love you.
Demonstrate your lovability.

"Divine Discontent"
leads you to "Divine Assignment".

"Divine Assignment"
leads to much abundance.

Light a candle
when you pray,
morning and evening.

What Does This Mean To You?
Spirit

_____

_____

_____

_____

_____

_____

_____

_____

_____

_____

_____

_____

_____

_____

_____

_____

_____

_____

_____

_____

_____

_____

_____

_____

God's arms are around you,
protecting you.
Feel His love.

When you keep God with you,
success is much easier.

"Ask and it shall be given.
Seek and you shall find.
Knock and it will be answered."

What Does This Mean To You?
Spirit

_____
_____
_____
_____
_____
_____
_____
_____
_____
_____
_____
_____
_____
_____
_____
_____
_____
_____
_____
_____
_____
_____
_____
_____
_____

You are not alone.
Talk to God,
then listen.

Surround yourself
with living plants
and loving animals.

Give up struggle.
Make God a way of living.

What Does This Mean To You?
Spirit

_____

_____

_____

_____

_____

_____

_____

_____

_____

_____

_____

_____

_____

_____

_____

_____

_____

_____

_____

_____

_____

_____

_____

You are a pinch of
God life.
Treat yourself with respect.

There is only surrender.
Healing takes place
when you surrender.

Tomorrow
is a brand new day.
God will be there
when you open your eyes.

What Does This Mean To You?
Spirit

_____

_____

_____

_____

_____

_____

_____

_____

_____

_____

_____

_____

_____

_____

_____

_____

_____

_____

_____

_____

_____

_____

_____

Your job is to keep
your God-given body
pure, clean, and holy.

The Hebrew word,
"El Shaddai"
means,
The God of More Than Enough.

Pray in reverence on your knees.
In your mind,
just stay there.

ACTIVITIES
&
JUST FOR FUN

Put on the music and
dance, dance, dance,
walk, walk, walk,
march, march, march.
Kick your feet,
reach up, bend down.

Moving your body
helps you breathe.
Breathing is important.

Walking every day
adds years to your life.
Do it twice a day.

Cancel the lawn service
and mow, rake, bend and carry.
Drink water all day.

Take a dance class,
or go swimming.
Get on a bicycle,
or go hike in a park.

Housework is a blessing.
It gets you moving and breathing
and it gives you a sense
of accomplishment.

Knowledge about food
is power.
Read lots of books on nutrition.

It's okay to take a nap
when you're in need.
No guilt.

Clean and polish;
wash and shine;
dust and sparkle.
Keep busy and do it all
for God.

Get or give yourself
a manicure.
If you can reach your toes,
a pedicure.

Buy a kit
to keep your hands busy
and your mind on the task.
Needlepoint, crewel, cross-stitch,
or sew on a button.
If this sounds torturous,
get a coloring book and color.

Paint something.
Paint something else.

Brush your teeth after meals,
instead of having dessert.

Make a daily to-do list
and cross off the items
as they are accomplished.

Take your time to
peruse the bookstore and
find something to read.
Take your time reading it.

Walk the dogs
or walk a neighbor to
get away from the fridge.

Spiritual community
is the best thing you can have
for yourself and your family.

Study and practice
an instrument
or a foreign language
to keep your mind
strong and active.

Tighten up
and
lighten up.

When the commercials come on,
get up and march
until the show returns.

I am breathing in.
I am breathing out.
I am breathing in.
I am breathing out.

JUST FOR FUN

Trust Yourself

Put a bowl of jelly beans on a table. RULE: No one may eat any for one week. Then, you may take just one. Create another RULE: No one may eat any for two weeks. Then you may eat two. Strengthen your character and have some fun. Engage others in the house or office to participate in this activity. See how long you can play the game. Stop before you get to 52 weeks and 52 jelly beans, so set a goal.

Another trust-yourself game is to buy a candy bar and keep it in your purse or on your desk for a month without eating it. Let everyone know the game. Challenge others to join in. Pretty soon, you'll forget that it's there. You win!

Spend a Day with an Orange

Pick a beautiful fresh orange and study it. Notice its color and rippley texture. Notice its belly button. Breathe in its essence. Begin to peel the orange and watch how its protective skin pulls away from the perfect sections inside. Listen to its sound while peeling it. Notice its intricacies and white stringy attachments. Remove one section, break its membrane and look at its little tear-drop shapes. Put the piece in your mouth slowly and savor its juices and flavor. Swallow and breathe. Remember that God made the orange trees for your sustenance and pleasure. Give thanks. Do the same with apple varieties, grapes, melons, kiwi, and star fruit.

This is an actual exercise in observing that I studied in my art classes. One assignment I had was to study a pebble for one week before I was to draw it. I memorized every bump, texture, and color distinctions in that pebble. God is so amazing.

Organize Your Space

Choose your most unruly closet. Empty all of its contents. Play spiritual music and feel you are doing this job for God. Paint it white so it looks clean and light and smells fresh. Before putting anything back, make sure it's clean and wearable. Get hangers you like and make sure they are all the same. Put your clothes on the hangers facing the same direction. Button the shirts, hang the pants upside down to maintain the crease. Hang t-shirts if you have room. Line up your shoes on a freshly cleaned closet floor, or get shoe shelves. Discard, donate, and cleanse. While you are busy with this project, drink water to keep from thinking about food every minute. You're getting a good workout by stretching, and bending, and lifting, and scrubbing. You're cleansing your body and purging things you don't need from your life. When you get rid of the old, you can then embrace the new. In the end, you will feel accomplished and much lighter.

Make Music

When going to yard sales, look for children's musical instruments like tambourines, drums, xylophones, cymbals, and so forth. Look on line at Craig's List or eBay for percussion instruments on sale. Gather your treasures and turn on your favorite music. Provide the accompaniment with your instruments. Spend at least a half hour playing and invite your family or friends to join you. Have a music party or gathering outside in the summer and lose yourself in the play.

Part Two

Stories, Poems, and Passions

A WEIGHTY QUESTION

To weigh, or not to weigh;
that is the question.

Before you begin your new diet program, you must weigh yourself so that you know how far you will have come. I know it's painful, but it will get better. If you can, have someone take pictures of you, as well. That should be enough to get you started. Put the pictures on the fridge.

Let's say you've been dieting for one week. We know that if you are able to stick to the program, you get the biggest drop right away. Now, if you weigh yourself and you've only lost two pounds, you might feel disappointed. You might think, "Why am I doing this? For a lousy two pounds? All this struggling and it doesn't really make much difference. I may as well eat."

PRAY FOR PATIENCE

Sometimes it happens that your body thinks it's starving and wants to hold onto the weight for a while, until it gets the message that you really are eating less, and it has to release the weight. So, if you've been dieting and you weigh yourself and you've gained weight or are on standby, you might think, "What's the point to dieting? I may as well eat."

PRAY FOR PATIENCE

If you forgot to count that brownie or cookies no one saw you take, then ...

PRAY FOR HONESTY

The best scenario is where you have been dieting and sticking to the program and you do lose significant pounds. Now, you might think, "Wow! I've lost a good amount of weight. So, it wouldn't hurt if I just had *a little bit* of those treats."

PRAY FOR CLARITY

I think it is best not to weigh yourself daily or weekly. I think the best strategy is to weigh once a month. Then, if you've made the commitment to yourself to be on a healthy program, and stayed the course, you are guaranteed to have lost. And, boy-o-boy, it is the best feeling. It's surprising and exhilarating. Then, you can ...

PRAY AND GIVES THANKS TO GOD FOR HIS LOVING CARE.

The answer to the question is, "Stay on the program and weigh monthly." If you don't agree, then do what you think best. Your opinion is as good as mine. And always ...

PRAY FOR STRENGTH

AMEN

IT WEIGHS ON ME

Do I take up too much space?

Do others see it round my face?

That extra piece of pie I ate,

already will decide my fate.

And what about the cake I had?

I told myself that I was bad.

It tasted good, and so it should.

But pie and cake are not so good.

Munch, crunch, swallow, clunk,

It weighs on me, it's just like junk.

THE ICE CREAM STORY

While working in my office, I got the nagging urge to put something in my mouth. My daughter had left the house with a friend, so I felt a false sense of freedom. Unfortunately, I developed a bad habit of eating mindlessly while working. I did make a rule (that I remembered later, after it was too late) that there would be no eating in the office. But then, no one was home except for the dogs, cat and bird. So, I meandered over to the fridge with that strawberry ice cream in mind. I should have thrown it out.

I'll measure out only a cup. Why measure? I can tell when I've eaten a cup. It's just like a scoop. So I took the entire half gallon into the office with a spoon. I had my fill and kept typing. I probably had about two scoops by then, but I was able to stop eating. Wheew! That was a close call. It could have been worse. "Next time measure, Gail," I said to myself.

I was about to put it back in the freezer, when I realized that my daughter and her friend had returned home. Oh, no! I couldn't take the tub into the kitchen where they were, because they would see me with it and I'd feel embarrassed and have to explain myself.

The ice cream had started to melt. I stared at it for more than a minute and decided that ice cream is no good when melted and re-frozen. So, I picked up the spoon and just scooped the melty part around the edges. By then, I probably had three scoops. Well, there was just a little bit left, so I finished it off.

I felt stuffed, sick, and stupid. Maybe I should make a magnet for the refrigerator that says, "Stick to the rules you make when you are in your right mind".

Dear God,
"Please give me the strength of mind to stick to the rules that I know are for my benefit. Let me feel you standing behind me. Please **help me put the spoon down**." Amen

POEM ABOUT FAT

Drat, drat, it's all 'bout fat.

It sticks to ma stomach, ma thighs, where I sat.

It's often called blubber, or grease, oil or lard.

When eaten too much, I'm excessively tared.

It's in the pur cow, who ends up on ma plate,

Whipped cream is so smooth, I simply can't wait.

Ma clothes just get tarter, I'm not any lyter,

Diets don't work, so this is ma fate.

Cow will not digest, unless it's cooked rare,

I've heard eatin' fat is good fer yer hair.

If not digested, I will get gas,

The worst thin' of all, it ends up on ma ass.

It's not just the cow, it's potater chips too,

Eatin' just one will simply not do.

The oil that's in peanuts is better, they say,

No more than one teaspoonful in a day.

I'm tared of fat; I'm tared of lard,

I'm tared of dietin' because it's so hard.

Oh, fiddle dee dee, I kin stand it no more,

If I keep eatin' fat, I won't get through that door.

THE BIGGEST LOSER

Each Sunday when I talk to my sister Rita, we always check on each other's weight and which diet we've tried that week. She loves trying new diets and cooking new recipes, especially the low-fat desserts. She usually gets down three pounds before she quits. I don't cook, so we always have good conversations.

Rita loves the show, THE BIGGEST LOSER because she finds it so inspirational. Some people actually lose 50 pounds in a week. Looking at all that fat makes me uncomfortable. It seems humiliating to me, as I imagine myself standing half-naked in front of a television audience. I just don't understand why they make people pull an airplane or dive in the mud. But to Rita, it shows hope.

Anyway, I watched it a few times and they showed this man who thought he should weigh 250 pounds, but the scale showed 252. So he says, "Wait a minute," and he moves the scale to another part of the floor. The scale still reads 252, so he turns it a bit and gets back on. Nope, it's still the same, so he moves it again. He weighs himself one more time and yes, it reads 250. He does the happy dance excitedly yelling, "250, I knew I was 250. Yeah!" I never laughed so hard because I've moved the scale myself.

Don't you wish we could lose two pounds by simply moving the scale? This story really makes the point about weighing. I can put on four pounds overnight. If I weigh myself every day, it plays havoc with my thoughts. I have found that even weighing every week is too much. If you tell yourself that you're going to follow your program and you do it, when you finally do weigh yourself after a month, you will be shocked at how much you have lost.

ÉCLAIRS

I passed up the éclairs today,

I knew I should,

Didn't know I could.

Then turned down the aisle,

With all the ice cream,

I was in a dream,

Swimming in ice cream.

Then came the cake,

I took the bait,

I thought it through,

"What's wrong with you?"

Along came pies,

Before my eyes,

Whipped cream on top,

I have to stop.

But why, why, why,

Can't I have that pie?

It's all so good,

I wish I could.

I have to pray,

"God guide my way,

Just get me through,

This maze of goo."

Finally, the cashier's line,

I take a breath,

And I feel fine.

Woo hoo, woo hoo,

I conquered goo,

To God I say,

"Thank you, thank you."

Fear and Motivation

It was on a TV night and I was flipping channels. I stopped on a show that was talking about being overweight. I couldn't believe what I was watching. There were several morbidly obese men and women who committed to a challenge. They signed a contract which said that they would each lose 60 pounds within the next three months, or a picture of them wearing a bikini would be put on the internet for all to see.

No one was told how to diet or exercise. No one was given any restrictions or directions. They were on their own. Before signing their contracts, each would pose for the photographer "bikini clad" and then decide if they would accept the challenge. While they changed into their suits, all we saw were shots of their legs and arms and terrified faces. To motivate them, that picture would become their desktop picture on their own computer staring back at them for the next six months. They all signed up.

What happened was amazing. I knew that all of them had been on various diets before, and had been unsuccessful. Everyone says that diets don't work, so why would they take the risk? They had tried so many times before and had repeatedly failed.

I breathlessly watched the participants shopping for healthy food, and cooking, and eating, and exercising on their own. I was feeling the fear factor, too. As each began to waiver and make excuses, they painfully pressed on. They had been struggling, and they all wanted to quit, but that picture was in front of them every day. They also had the others for support to keep them going.

Every one of them made their goal weight within the time frame, except for Jill, who was only 2 pounds away from her target. She said that she didn't care if her picture went on the internet because she felt and looked so good now, and it was all worth it. The host of the show kindly tore up her picture.

Why did it work this time? What was their secret? Was it simply fear that kept them on the diet of their choice? Was it the exercise they did every day, hour after hour? Was it their support of each other that created a bond to help them tough it out? Perhaps, it was the commitment they made to themselves to doing something they wanted to do and seeing it through. Whatever the combination, it worked for them.

It was an interesting and funny experiment in how fear can affect us. If the doctors told us that we had to lose weight as a matter of life or death, we probably would control our diets and exercise better than we do now. That would be fear, and yet some people don't do it, even in that circumstance. But, how can we adapt the outcome of this story to our own situation in order to find success? Could a constant commitment to God become our motivating factor? Instead of fear, we could certainly find a healthier lifestyle. Instead of fear, we could find support from others for our commitment. Instead of fear, we could find God's love.

Are you up for the challenge?

Roll the cameras!

A PURPOSE, A PASSION, AND A PLAN

What is your purpose in life? Why were you put on Earth? What is it you are here to do? Is it more than one thing? Is it a series of things? This is our "Divine Discontent". It is that nagging urge to do something special; a "blessed unrest" is how Martha Graham put it. It keeps us searching for that meaning to life; that "Divine Assignment" from God. What does God want me to do?

How many times have you felt this restlessness or heard these restless thoughts in your head? Have you figured it out, yet? Why is it appropriate to ask these questions in a book about staying on your diet?

I believe that if we don't find our passion, something that is so important to our heart and soul, something that gives us a sense of accomplishment, it's as though we are wandering through the desert for 40 years without direction. If we don't have a plan to keep us busy and enlightened and excited with our lives, we will continue to stuff our faces with bad foods. We may be trying to fill up an uncomfortable void that we are feeling.

Every time I start a new job or a project that I can throw myself into, I lose weight. My adrenalin always kicks into first gear, and it is the fuel that keeps me running fast and furiously. I consume myself in what I am doing and get so involved that I actually must remind myself to eat. Can you imagine that? It happened again when I started writing this book. I lost 16 pounds.

When you have a passion, it is what you think about most of the time. It breaks through the "I can't do it" thinking, and puts you on the path of forward movement and excitement toward an accomplishment. The Source can create anything and is your partner in everything. If you knew your partner in your project was *All Powerful,* there would be no fear in going forward. Think of your passion as your "Divine Assignment" by God.

If you have not yet discovered your passion, and don't have a plan, there are many books available to help you in your discovery. I've read a large number of them. I was searching for a long time. Here is a list to get you started on your quest:

The Purpose of Your Life
Carol Adrienne

Creating a Life Worth Living
Carol Lloyd

Live the Life You Love
Barbara Sher

Do What You Love and The Money Will Follow
Marsha Sinetar

To Build the Life You Want, Create the Work You Love
Marsha Sinetar

I Could Do Anything If I Only Knew What It Was
Barbara Sher

Finding Your Perfect Work
Paul and Sarah Edwards

There are so many great ideas in these books that will ignite your spirit. Please e-mail me with success stories, so I can share your excitement with those who take my Spiritual Diet Seminars.

http://www.CreativeVisionsPublishing.com
My e-mail address is Gail@CreativeVisionsPublishing.com.
Hope to hear from you.

Part Three

Prayers

From the Sanskrit
A Salutation of the Dawn

Look to this day,

For it is life,

The very life of life.

In its brief course,

Be all the verities and realities

Of your existence:

The bliss of growth,

The glory of action,

The splendor of beauty.

For yesterday is already a dream,

And tomorrow is only a vision.

But today, well lived,

Makes every yesterday,

A dream of happiness,

And every tomorrow,

A vision of hope.

Look well, therefore to this day.

Such is the Salutation of the Dawn.

As I Open My Eyes

Dear Lord,

As I open my eyes this new day,

I can feel Your Presence about me.

I ask that You be my strength today,

and carry me,

so that I am not so weary.

My desire for food is overwhelming.

I ask that You be my only desire.

Help me be Your devoted one,

and choose only You.

Amen

Thinking about Food

Dear God,

Please help me stop thinking

about food all the time.

Please release me from my constant cravings

and quiet my mind.

Let me feel you beside me

and grant me peace.

Amen

Help with Food

Dear God,

Help! I need help with food.

Help me to choose the food that is

healthy and holy,

created by You,

and given to the Earth's creatures,

as a gift of nourishment and sustenance.

Before I eat,

show me its beauty and simplicity

of Godliness.

Amen

I Give Up

Dear God.

I give up! I can no longer live like this.

I hate what I've done to this body,

You have blessed me with.

I want to be your faithful child,

and surrender to your natural laws.

Amen

Fat Food and Healthy Food

Beautiful Lord,

Please help me know which foods make me
unhealthy and fat,

and which foods make me
healthy and strong.

Please dissipate my desires for the foods
that are not good for me,

and desire those that are good.

Help me determine when I am hungry
and when I am not.

Let me do these things with ease and assurance,
not with struggle and resistance.

Help me use my life to demonstrate
Your gentle power.

Amen

Hold Me in Your Loving Arms

Dear Lord, Creator of all that is,

Who has given us Your wonderful food

for our sustenance and pleasure.

I kneel down before you, dear Lord,

and am humbled by Your greatness and goodness.

I surrender to You my will and

I ask for Your guidance throughout the day.

Please help me with my food choices,

and stay with me

as You hold me in Your loving arms.

Amen

Centered in You

Dear God,

When I go to the fridge,

help me stop and get centered in You.

When I open it

I will imagine that you are

standing beside me,

helping me with every decision

I must make.

Please guide me to reach for

the nourishing food

and leave the rest alone.

Amen

Going to Work Today

Dear God,

When I go to work today,

please help me say, "no thank you"

to all the fattening goodies

that someone has baked especially for our office.

Help me to easily pass

on the birthday cake and pizza,

the cookies and chocolate,

the chips and dips.

Let it be easy, because I know that

You are beside me and won't let me go.

Amen

Try One More Time

Dear Heavenly Father,

Thank you for giving me

the courage and strength

to try one more time

to become the healthy and pure person

You created.

Amen

I Made a Mistake

Dear Loving Spirit,

I slipped from my goal today,

and I know it's okay to make a mistake.

Please help me follow

the healthy path.

Help me to notice

when I am not hungry.

Help me make positive choices

when I am.

Amen

Fighting with Food

Dear Beautiful Lord,

I ask that You

please set me free from the prison

of fighting with food.

Help me to release temptations and desires

and choose health and lightness.

I ask that You empower me with discipline

and help me overcome any obstacles

I might face today.

Amen

I'm Feeling Separated

Dear God,

I know You are there,

but I have felt so separated from You.

Help me to see clearly

that my body does not need so much food.

I know I could feel closer to You

if I ate better and ate less.

Please give me Your blessing today

and stand by me when I open the fridge,

so that I will know You are with me.

Amen

Focus on My Health

Dear Loving Creator,

Please clear my thinking,

and help me focus on my health.

Breathe Your strength into me

and surround me with

Your light.

Amen

No Cheating Today

Dear Loving God,

I made it through the day today with no cheating.

I stayed on my program and followed the plan.

I ate less, made good choices, and kept alert.

It's working (woohoo) and I am hopeful.

Thank You, thank You, thank You.

I love you, my beautiful God,

and know I will be successful this time.

Amen

I'm Going to Do It

Dear Heavenly One,

Today, I'm going to do it.

I will make healthy choices,

I will take a long walk,

I will drink lots of water.

I will set an activity goal

and follow through.

I will do it because I want to

commit to my faith in You.

Amen

Sweet, Chewy, Salty, and Greasy

Dear God,

Help!

I want to eat, eat, eat!

I want sweet and chewy,

I want salty and greasy.

I want ice cream!!!

I know I can't continue on this path.

Help me to know that

following You

leads to health and peace.

Amen

Feeling Defeated

Dear God,

I've already ruined my day.

I feel so defeated.

Please give me the clarity of thought

to get back on track, now.

I want to honor You.

I will recommit my love.

Amen

Calm My Rush for Food

Dear Lord of my soul,

Please teach me patience.

Calm my rush for food

and instant gratification.

Calm my mind.

Let me stop to breathe

and to think

about what I really need.

Thank you, thank you, thank you.

Amen

I'm Feeling Hopeful and Strong

Dear Spirit of Light,

Thank you God

for the weight I am losing.

It is a new beginning

of health and restoration.

I am feeling hopeful and strong,

beautiful and healthy,

more in control of my life.

Thank you for your gentle touch.

I am on my way

and I am excited.

Amen

I Am Losing Weight

Dear God,

I am losing weight

and it feels great.

Feeling Your presence

makes it easy and sweet.

I feel good about what I am doing,

and excited about the future.

I love You, Lord.

Thank You for being here with me.

I know all I have to do

is ask You in.

Amen

I Have Now Learned

Dear God,

I have now learned

that when I feel hungry,

bored, or unhappy,

if I will just stop, and breathe,

and think of You,

I can feel Your Love,

and know You are with me.

Thank You, Father.

I love you.

Amen

The Day is Done

Dear Father,

The day is done.

I kept you with me today

through all the rushing and noise.

I concentrated on being productive

instead of being hungry.

I kept my efforts to myself

and only shared my struggles with You.

Thank you for being there.

Each new day

is a day spent with You.

Amen

Beautiful Spirit

Father God,

Creator of the Universe,

Ruler of my Soul,

Teacher of my Mind,

Protector of my Body,

Lover of my Spirit,

Knower of my Life,

Please quiet my mind.

Help me to focus my thoughts

on what I need to do today,

and what is acceptable to you.

Let my mind calm my body,

let me stop to breathe,

to spend a moment thinking of You,

to pray for others.

Please release me from my

fears and tears and worries,

and know that your arms

are around me,

enveloping me in Your love.

Thank you, Beautiful Spirit.

Amen

Part Four

Your Journal

Journaling

Some people like to write, some don't. I urge those who don't to please use the journal which follows. Its content concerns your emotional experiences around food and diets. I believe that if you work with this journal, your mindset will become clear, which will then lead to healing your thinking about why you may be unhealthy and overweight.

Journaling helps us to make clear and conscious choices about the way we live our lives. Since we have a finite time on Earth, we must fill our precious time with quality, productivity, and contribution to others and ourselves. We must not fill our time with, as Marianne Williamson says, "watching bad TV and eating bad food".

Sometimes it's hard to remember that each decision we make all day long involves God. Can we make better decisions about our bodies than the one who created them? If we think that we can do better than God, we are not in our purest form.

"Not mine, but Your will be done".

The questions in this next exercise may be hard to think about, but if you try, I think you will receive enlightening information about how you got where you are today. As we all know, becoming healthy and losing weight is not easy. We must use all the tools we can work with to achieve our optimum quality of life. How badly do you want the ultimate best life has to offer? I especially want to enjoy the best life for myself, my family, and my friends, and I want it for you, too. So, let's get to work.

Describe your personal vision of God?

What is your background with religion and God? How does it manifest in your life, today?

Do you consider yourself to be a pious person? How do you display it?

Have you ever felt the presence of God? How did this Power appear to you?

What things are you grateful for?

What is your life about at this time?

What do you want your life's mission to be?

What are your unfulfilled dreams? Are you still dreaming?

What are your fears? Are they debilitating?

What problems are weighing you down?

How does food fit into your life? Are you around it all day or do you have to go get it?

Do you pray about eating and food?

Have any family members been ill because of weight issues? Please explain.

What messages did your family give you about food?

How do you eat? Are you standing, sitting at a table, grazing all day? Are you unconscious? Do you wait until you're starving or do you eat one big meal and several small ones?

Do you consider yourself a food addict? Why?

What are your food addictions?

What are your triggers? Boredom, loneliness, depression, stress, self-nurturing, fear, rejection, oblivion, hopelessness, success, happiness, or some other feeling?

Were you ever thin? Were you healthy then? What were your eating and exercise patterns at that time?

Why do you overeat? When did your food issues start?

List all the foods that make you fat.

List your excuses and negotiations about overeating.

Do you exercise? What do you do?

What have others said about your body? Do you believe what they tell you?

What weight-loss programs have you tried? Which ones were successful for you? What did you like about them?

Describe the feeling of being hungry.

Describe the feeling of being full.

What do you like about dieting?

What would keep you from failing again?

Could you commit to joining a support group? How would you find one that you would be comfortable with?

List your successes in life.

What were you hoping to get from buying this book?

What parts do you think are most helpful?

Do you have any thoughts of other Minders that could be added to any of the sections?

I would love to hear from you if you are willing to share those thoughts with me, so that I can share them with others? Write to me with your suggestions and I will send you a free gift. Please e-mail me at:

Gail@SpiritualDietSeminars.com
or
Gail@CreativeVisionsPublishing.com

Part Five

Bunches of Things to Do Besides Eating

Our Sedentary Lifestyle

According to Wikipedia, "Our sedentary lifestyle is most common to the modern western cultures. It is characterized by remaining inactive for most of the day with little or no exercise. It is a factor in obesity, type 2 diabetes, heart disease, depression, hemorrhoids, muscle atrophy, and a weak immune system function."

Remember when people used to:

Get up and change the channel on their television instead of using the remote? Up and down they went all day long. They worked their abs and leg muscles.

Type on a typewriter instead of using a computer? You had to push those keys and throw the carriage working your fingers and arms.

Walk to the corner drugstore and back instead of driving, or walk to and from school? Aerobic activity.

Use the stairs instead of taking the elevator? People do that now. Very Aerobic and builds your leg and butt muscles.

Wash and dry our own dishes instead of using the dishwasher?

Hand wash delicates and sweaters instead of using the delicate cycle on the washing machine?

Hang our laundry outside to dry instead of using the dryer? Getting outside on a nice day was wonderful.

Iron our clothes and bed linens? It made me feel like a princess to wear crisp clean clothes and get into a freshly ironed bed.

Wash our own windows and screens? That is an activity that involves reaching and bending and being outside.

Push our own lawn mowers instead of using a gas or electric mower, or hiring a service? That was hard physical labor.

Shovel the snow and rake the leaves instead of using blowers or hiring a service? More hard work.

Sew our own clothes, costumes for Halloween, curtains, and even doll clothes instead of buying them? You crafty person.

Make a snowman, instead of buying the new and improved blow-up kind? Actually playing with the family and friends.

Have a snowball fight, play badminton, volleyball, or Jump rope? Jump in a pile of raked leaves?

Wash and vacuum your own car? You can do it better than the car wash. Then tip yourself.

Open the garage door manually instead of pushing a button?

Clean our own floors on our hands and knees instead of using the push pads?

Sweep the dirt off of the sidewalks? Yes, my father did it.

Carry fire wood and make a real fire instead of lighting the gas?

Park in the furthest spot instead of the closest? Okay, no one used to do that, but let's do it now.

Let's get with it devoted health seekers, rather than take the easy way. Fortunately, I have compiled a list of Bunches of Things to Do Besides Eating. Don't just read it and laugh. Pick something and do it.

In fact, I would love to hear from those of you who have thought of other things we used to do. Again, there is a free gift waiting for you if you can add to this list. Please write to me at:

Gail@CreativeVisionsPublishing.com or
Gail@SpiritualDietSeminars.com

BUNCHES OF THINGS TO DO
BESIDES EATING

1. Have a tasty diet drink (I prefer peach ice tea), cold water, iced coffee, or a flavorful diet soda. They will fill you up and give you a refreshing feeling. Have warm tea in the cold weather to feel cozy.

2. Go outside and take a walk. Take your dogs or walk with a friend. Group walks are easier to schedule with neighbors. Remember the Indian Princess Summerfall Winterspring on the Howdy Doody Show? Dress for the weather. Each season has its God given beauty, and it's all for you to enjoy.

3. Buy fresh flowers or a plant for your home. Surround yourself with beautiful living things. They are not expensive at the super stores, and they soothe your soul.

4. Walk the treadmill, elliptical, ride a bike, or skate with protective gear. Do something twice a day to increase your metabolism. Consult with your doctor and be careful.

5. Cut the grass, rake the leaves, or shovel the snow. Again, consult with a doctor. You can save money by canceling the service and get exercise at the same time. You will be communing with nature, and that brings you closer to Spirit.

6. In the fall, find beautiful leaves of all colors and shapes to press, or flowers to dry. When I was in school, we used to put them in a book and label them. Now, I put them in frames as botanical art.

7. Brush your teeth, wash your hands and face, or take a bath or shower. Cleansing helps you relax and gets you in touch with your purified self.

8. Breathe deeply and slowly ten times. Say in your mind, "I am breathing in, I am breathing out." Then you have time to think if you still want sugar, starch, and grease, or a healthy snack.

9. Bend forward at the waist and hang with your elbows on your thighs. Tuck your chin to your chest. This stretches your spine. I always hear cricks and cracks when I do it, and it feels so good. Push yourself up to standing position by putting your hands on your thighs.

10. Chew on celery, carrots, cherry tomatoes, cucumbers, or sour pickles. I find that sour pickles take away my sweet cravings. They have very few calories and it keeps your mouth busy.

11. Chew on sugar-free gum or candies to take your mind off eating. Better yet, munch on fruit crisps apples and pears or a handful of healthy nuts. That actually helped me stop smoking many years ago.

12. Pick a room and clean a shelf. Take everything off the shelf and wash it down. Dust, vacuum or wash items on it and decide what you don't want and begin a pile for give-away. Throw out what is not useful to anyone. Organize and return the items to the shelf in a lovely design. Try another one, but don't over-do it so that it begins to feel like a chore.

13. Get or give yourself a manicure or pedicure, if you can reach your toes. When I was much heavier, my breasts and stomach were too big for me to reach my toes and still breathe. There was too much fat on my middle to bend. So, out of necessity, I began getting pedicures. Although, I could not really afford it at the time, it made me feel pampered and cared for. It has since become an enjoyable splurge. Guess what? Men can get manicures and pedicures, too. How nice for their ladies.

14. Ladies, shave your legs and pluck your eyebrows. I know it's bothersome, but it will give you something to do while not eating. It will also make you feel much better about yourself.

15. Here is one adventure. Shop for wallpaper. You don't have to buy it or need it, but some of the papers are so beautiful that I feel like I'm looking at art work. You may find a beautiful remnant that you could use to cover a box. Yes, it's a craft, but you won't be eating and you will be doing something creative. It will also get you out of the house.

16. Ever heard of the Hula Hoop? Many of us used to twirl them in the 1950s. I was so good at it then, I could easily go forever. Now is a different story. Get two of them at a children's toy store, so you can play with a friend. There are even classes in hooping. It's not easy, but don't give up. Instead of heading to the fridge during commercials, pick up the Hula Hoop and give it a whirl.

17. Join a community theater troupe. You don't have to act, sing or dance. You can participate by helping with scenery or costumes, and you'll be playing with fun people and connecting with community.

18. Shop for new knobs for a dresser or for closet doors. New knobs can make a whole room look new, and it may inspire you to do other updates.

19. Take everything, everything, everything out of your bathroom, including all items in the cabinets and closets and drawers. Let's clean. Begin cleaning by getting rid of the cobwebs at the ceiling and work your way down. Get rid of old, discolored, torn, disgusting towels. Fold and arrange the nice ones beautifully, in case someone using the bathroom peeks. Wash and clean every bottle as if it were an assignment from God. It will keep you busy moving and reaching and breathing and sweating. Drink lots of water while you work. Don't forget the spiritual music.

20. Look through all your magazines, or have your friends save their old ones for you. Create a dream binder by cutting out the pages that are of interest to you and categorize them. Put each category you choose in the binder. I collect beautiful colors from ads in magazines that I like for the time when I am ready to paint a room. Other categories I enjoy are fashion, decorated rooms that I find attractive, and places I'd like to travel.

21. Create your "Dream Board" by using words and pictures from magazines of something you've always wanted to do. Create a montage or a collage. I love collecting pictures of animals, faces of babies, or just smiling faces. I made a board which inspires my dream of writing a musical theater production one day. I put it in a poster frame for viewing and it reminds me of what is in my heart, and what is possible.

22. Buy and use an exercise DVD for walking, dancing, kick boxing, tap dancing, belly dancing, or something new and exciting. There are a bazillion of them, even though my accountant says there is no such number.

23. Something I rarely do is wash the light fixtures and the windows. It really brightens a room, and could brighten your mood. Do just one and see if you like the effect.

24. Paint something with crazy colors: a tray, a wall, a chair, an old dresser, or even a picture. I found a chair on garbage day and painted it bright red. Everyone loved it so much, they wanted it for their own.

25. Write an old fashioned letter on pretty stationery to someone you think about, but never call. Reconnecting with a friend gives you and them a good feeling.

26. Address envelopes for your holiday card list early.

27. Write a heart-felt letter to God. Talk to Him about everything. Keep it with you so you can review it regularly. If you don't want anyone to see it, shred it.

28. Write a story you remember about your childhood. Doing something difficult is good for your brain. Pretend it is a school assignment, or better yet, think of it as a memory book to pass on to your family, if you so wish. If you're intimidated writing, talk into a tape recorder and transcribe it. It would be quite an accomplishment, don't you think?

29. Put on your favorite vocalist and sing along, even if you can't sing. Make sure you are in a comfortable place where there is no one to criticize you. I sing in the car when I'm alone. Pretend you have an audience that is giving you a swelling applause. Then take a bow.

30. If you have plants or flowers, re-pot them with fresh soil. Wash their leaves. Surround yourself with beauty and God's living things.

31. Help a neighbor, talk to the elderly, or play with a child. Color with them in a coloring book. Do something helpful for others.

32. Stay current on your bills and checkbook. Organize your papers monthly to be ready for tax time in advance.

33. Give your dog or cat a bath and a good brushing. Even if they don't like it, they'll be clean and pretty. They'll get more hugs and kisses from you and you'll get more kisses from them.

34. I love to read the Yellow Pages. I get so many good ideas for things I need or want to do. It's amazingly informative.

35. Organize your books and music by categories and then by artists. Next time you look for something, you'll be able to find it more easily.

36. Get out of the house, or away from work, and go to the card shop. Spend some time reading the cards and buy one for a special person.

37. Join a community group or church or temple. Become a volunteer for an organization that helps others. Make a list and research each organization on the internet.

38. Peruse the bookstore for a few hours. There are wonderful picture books in the children's section, as well as teaching and educational books. I buy them for children I know. Every area has something to see. Travel, decorating, and architecture are some of my interests.

39. There are many spiritual books and books of prayer. It is important to use a book of prayers to get you up in the morning and put you to bed at night. Find the ones with which you resonate. Buy a book and enjoy.

40. Collect cartoon favorites from the Sunday newspapers and make a scrapbook. Whenever you add a new one, you can read them all and chuckle. Put it on the coffee table and share it with friends, giving them a chuckle, too.

41. Go to the craft store and pick just one thing to do. For me, it's like being a kid in a candy shop, or just like being *ME* in a candy shop, only it's not fattening. It's full of imagination and colors and shapes and textures and dreams. They have classes, too.

42. Build a support group around work, such as, those wanting to start their own business, or build a web-site to sell things. What do you dream about doing?

43. A fabulous e-site is Yahoogroups.com. There are support groups on *everything*, including weight loss or spiritual weight loss or spirituality or self-growth. Explore and connect. The whole world is yours.

44. You can go to the movies by yourself at any time.

45. Make "life lists" to help you get clear:

Things you want to do,

Things you want to have,

Things you love,

Places you want to go,

Self-improvement in body, mind, and Spirit,

How your relationships might be strengthened,

List your strengths.

46. Go to garage sales and yard sales. I've found many inexpensive treasures and my friends will tell you that my home is stuffed full of lovely things. It is play time for me and I enjoy talking to people.

47. Have a garage sale and clear out all the things you no longer love or have a need for. Make some money and have fun playing with people. At my last sale, people asked me, "How much for this piece?" When I said, "Oh, that's $9.98", they thought it was so funny. It's a lot of work, but I invited my friends to sit with me and talk and eat apples and walnuts and drink ice water. I know it is food, but it's good food and good friends. I made $100 and had a great day.

48. Organize your photos. Throw out the bad ones. What are you saving them for? I filled two garbage bags to the top. This is a very involved and time-consuming project to keep you busy and feeling good. Have fun. Buy new albums and organize by time periods, trips, and celebrations. Scrap booking is very popular now, and there are so many related stickers and three-dimensional items that will make your pictures come alive. You can put pictures on your computer, too.

49. There is a great new software program that transfers all your cassette tapes and vinyl records onto CDs. There is also a more expensive alternative to the software which has the capacity to do the same thing in a simpler way. It looks like an old fashioned record player and it can also be used to play your audio media.

50. Take classes. Every community center has lots of classes from which to choose. There are exercise classes, like yoga or tap. Don't laugh. Ever heard of "The Tapping Grannies"? They are all in their 70s and are fabulous. If they can do it, you can do it. There are multitudes of art classes, like glass, jewelry, painting, sculpting, and photography. There are Toastmaster classes and computer classes just for you, as well.

51. Join a book club and make new friends. If you're too busy with work, create an activity to do when it is break time or lunch time or after work for a half hour. When I worked at a bank, I offered to teach a jazz dance class on Saturday mornings. Everyone loved it and it was great exercise.

52. Become an expert on something you love to do and set up an on-line business. Go to a few sites that do everything for you: sitebuildit.com, godaddy.com, cafepress.com. There are many and you can make additional income, instead of spending it on food that is not good for you.

53. Every Sunday morning, my sister Rita cuts out coupons for the supermarket. It's a smart way to save a bit of money. She also looks through Suzanne Somers' dessert book, *Somersize Desserts,* before she leaves for the market and gets the ingredients to make a non-fattening treat for herself. What a plan!

54. According to the experts, the best thing you can do for your mind is to learn a new language or learn to play an instrument. You only need to buy a keyboard to learn how to play the piano. Just think of learning three songs well and entertaining your friends for some grand applause. Also, this kind of practice develops new paths of brain activity and keeps you alert.

55. Write your memoirs. No one ever has to see it, but the exercise may be enlightening. It could also be something to pass down to your family if you wish.

56. Make a list of all the funny things your pets do and frame their pictures with their personality profile. I have three shi tuz pups, a cat, and a screaming colorful bird.

57. The bookstore has many different kinds of workbooks to explore. Some subjects are on strengthening your marriage, raising your children, communicating with yourself, and your right work. Find your interest and spend some time exploring and learning.

58. Take everything off your bed, and throw it in the wash. For me, it takes about five loads, but I love doing it. It feels so wonderful to climb into a fresh and comfortable bed. Sweet dreams.

59. Practice meditating. It is so important for your mental health. This is how I do it. First I turn off all the electronics. I light a candle in a jar and find a quiet space to sit comfortably. I close my eyes and concentrate on my breathing. I breathe in deeply, and breathe out deeply. The way I clear my mind is to say, "I am breathing in, I am breathing out, I am breathing in, I am breathing out." I do this for about five minutes before praying. This time is for you and God.

60. Everyone has files in a file cabinet. Go through each file. You may find treasures or you will be relieved to throw out papers that you no longer want. If you don't have a file cabinet, get one. Put an end to your piles and simplify your life.

61. Drive to a park or a lake. Take a blanket and a book, or a camera. Go alone or take a friend and enjoy the view. My friend, Paulette, goes to the lake with her dog, Scarletta, so that her dog can swim. She talks to others who have brought their dogs and they have an enjoyable time.

62. Spend a day at a museum. It is indeed a place that wakes up your ancient spirit from times gone by. Every community has something wonderful to see.

63. In your journal, list everything that you are grateful for and everything at which you have been successful. Write some prayers and visit your book often, adding to it.

64. Have a party. Ask your guests to bring a game to play. Many of us have lost that "play with your friends" time. Remember Monopoly, Checkers, Old Maid, Go Fish, Scrabble? It really can be like childhood fun.

65. Have a Karaoke party and sing, sing, sing. There are special karaoke machines with microphones and music just for your singing pleasure. It's a great way to have fun, fun, fun.

66. Pace, march, or kick your feet while talking on the phone. It keeps you breathing and in movement.

67. Empty your purse or briefcase and clean it out.

68. Keep your environment safe by cleaning out the refrigerator and cupboards. Get rid of the things that tempt you and replace them with healthy choices.

69. Recycle your old clothes like they used to do in the olden times. Cut them up and sew them together for an interesting quilted blanket, a throw, or shawl. I save velour and silky items for my future blanket project.

70. Collect quotes of wisdom and keep a special journal for them. Add poems you like, too.

71. Buy fresh beautiful flowers for your bedroom and every room in the house.

72. Say, "I love you" as much as you can.

Part Six

Resources to Use

RECOMMENDED BOOK LIST AND AUTHORS

YOU on a DIET
The Owner's Manual for Waist Management
Michael F. Roizen, M.D. and Mehmet C. Oz, M.D.
This is explains a lot about health and your body.

Prevention Magazine's Nutrition Advisor
The Ultimate Guide to the Health-Boosting
and Health-Harming Factors in Your Diet
Mark Bricklin
Over 1,000 Foods Analyzed & Rated

Hungry Girl
Recipes, Survival Strategies,
Guilt-Free Eating, Great Food Swaps
Lisa Lillien

8 Minutes in the Morning
An Official 3 Hour Diet Fitness Plan
Jorge Cruise

Dr. Atkins New Diet Revolution
Robert Atkins
High protein, low carbohydrate diet

Somersize Desserts
30 Fantastic Recipes For Sumptuous,
Great Tasting, Guilt-Free Treats
Suzanne Somers

Daily Word for Weight Loss
Spiritual Guidance To Give You Courage On Your Journey
Colleen Zuck and Elaine Meyer

Breaking Free From Emotional Eating
An End to the Anguish of Emotional Eating
Geneen Roth

The Spiritual Path Guidebook
Suggestions and Reminders That will Support You
In Creating Your Own Reality
I have purchased this for gifts a hundred times.
Dick Stutphen

Everyday Wisdom
Dr. Wayne Dyer
A pocket-book about inner wisdom
This is a good take-along book for when you're waiting
somewhere. I don't leave home without taking a book.

Illuminated Prayers
Marianne Williamson
A lovely gift-book of prayers

One Minute Prayers to Begin and End Your Day
Hope Lyda
A gift book of prayers based on Biblical quotes

RECOMMENDED WEBSITES:

www.Beliefnet.com
Norris Chumbley has lots to say about faith and diet.

www.Yahoogroups.com
This is an amazing site to find a support group for anything
in which you are interested. Chat with others about your subject
of interest.

www.selfawareness.com
Steven S. Sadleir gives guided meditations in his
"24-hour Enlightenment Radio" show.

www.freemeditations.com
Instructions on how to meditate and attain inner peace and
freedom.

www.MarianneWilliamson.com
It is my humble opinion that Marianne is one of the most brilliant
minds on the planet today. She speaks and writes on spirituality.

www.bestdietforme.com
A list of the top 60 diet programs along with quizzes about food
and nutrition.

www.50millionpounds.com
A diet and health challenge.

www.HayHouseRadio.com
This is inspirational talk radio featuring authors published by Hay House.

www.oprah.com
Dr. Oz is on this site with health advice.

www.b-wire.com
Support and people to talk with and share concerns.

www.weightwatchers.com
Thoughts on food choices, support groups, and recipes.

www.CreativeVisionsPublishing.com
My own website with my Miraculously Memorable Minder™ Cards, a Pocket Minder, magnets, mugs, mousepads, calendars, t-shirts, tote bags and books. More to come as it develops and grows. Please be patient with me and my computer skills.

About the Author

Gail M. Freid has been an Ordained Minister and Practitioner with The International Metaphysical Ministry in Sedona, Arizona since 1994. In October of 1996, she received her Certification for Advanced Studies in Pastoral Psychology. In 1999, she attended the Church of Today Unity's Ministerial Program presented by Marianne Williamson. Unity, now named Renaissance Unity, is located in Warren, Michigan.

There she became a student of Reverend Jack Boland, Dr. Wayne Dyer, Jack Canfield, Mark Victor Hansen, Les Brown, John Gray, and the many personal growth and Spiritual teachers who spoke and gave workshops at the church. Renaissance Unity is considered to be one of the largest "new thought" churches in the country.

Ms. Freid graduated from Oakland University in Rochester, Michigan with a Certification in Secondary Education. She loved teaching High School English Literature, Poetry, Grammar, and Theater.

Her writing and Public Relations career was focused in radio and television with local celebrities for many years. Gail made a transition to the corporate world of Financial Consultation, where she won many awards and conducted many seminars for clients, while winning their trust and respect. She discovered her passion in writing, teaching, and art, music and dance and now pursues her dreams.

Most of all, Gail loves God and believes we can use His strength to create a healthier life. Because she struggles with weight and health, like many people in America, she began writing prayers and Minders to help her stay on her diet program and kept them in her purse. She was so inspired that her writings grew into this book.

The Beginning

3608671

Made in the USA